ROMAN
BRITAIN

Richard Russell Lawrence

SHIRE LIVING HISTORIES

How we worked • How we played • How we lived

First published in Great Britain in 2010 by Shire
Publications Ltd, Midland House, West Way, Botley,
Oxford OX2 0PH, United Kingdom.
44-02 23rd Street, Suite 219, Long Island City, NY11101,
USA.

E-mail: shire@shirebooks.co.uk   www.shirebooks.co.uk

A CIP catalogue record for this book is available from the
British Library.

Shire Living Histories no. 1 • ISBN-13: 978 0 74780 778 0

Richard Russell Lawrence has asserted his right under the
Copyright, Designs and Patents Act, 1988, to be identified
as the author of this book.

Designed by Myriam Bell Design, France and typeset in
Perpetua and Gill Sans.
Printed in China through Worldprint Ltd.

10 11 12 13 14   10 9 8 7 6 5 4 3 2 1

COVER IMAGE
Reconstruction of Wroxeter – street scene outside the
market hall (forum opposite). Artwork by Ivan Lapper.

ACKNOWLEDGEMENTS
Bath and North East Somerset Council, pages 70 and 72;
Bridgeman Art Library, pages 8 (bottom), 29, 31, 32
(top), 44 (both), 48 (bottom), 57 (bottom), 59, 64 (top),
76, and 77; Trustees of the British Museum, page 69;
English Heritage Photo Library, cover and pages 25, 42,
and 50–1; Helen Goff, page 12; Museum of London, page
56; Nagamoto Mari, page 4; National Roman Army
Museum, page 41; Niki Odolphie, page 11 (bottom); Shire
Publications (Pete Crooks) pages 26–7; Topfoto pages 10,
15, 16, 18, 24 (top), 36, 48 (top), 53, and 57; Wessex
Archaeology, pages 6, 14 (top), 19 (top), 22, 24 (bottom),
32 (bottom), 33 (bottom), 38 (bottom), 41 (top), and 49
(both); D. White Architectural Photographs, Cornell
University Library, page 8 (top). All other photographs
and artwork from the author's collection.

Shire Publications is supporting the Woodland Trust, the UK's leading woodland conservation charity, by funding the dedication of trees.

CONTENTS

PREFACE

BOOKS ON ROMAN BRITAIN are – to coin a phrase – legion, and range from detailed archaeological reports to lurid accounts of the thrills and spills of the gladiatorial arena. Everyone knows something of the impact the Romans had here, with their roads, towns, walls still forming the backdrop of Britain today.

The vast majority of books on Roman Britain written for the general reader concentrate on life in these highly visible zones, whether in the chilly forts along the length of Hadrian's Wall, or in the great healing and religious complex of Aquae Sulis or the burgeoning cities of Londinium and Eburacum. Nor is this surprising when we recall that these three sites, as Bath, London and York, have played and continue to play a huge role in the British sense of the past.

This book, as part of the Shire Publications Living Histories series, tries to move beyond these great centres of Roman civilisation, to investigate what life was like for the ordinary inhabitant of Roman Britain: a farmer or a craftsman in a smaller town; not an immigrant soldier from southern Europe but a native Briton for whom the Roman way of life was – initially at least – unfamiliar. The author explores how such people lived, how far they were forced into changing their lifestyles, economically if not militarily, and how much they accepted the new ways to which they had to accommodate themselves.

It looks at the daily round, the food and drink, the work patterns, the cycle of life, of ordinary Britons, and also of the 'Romans' – who might in fact have been born almost anywhere across Europe or the Mediterranean world – alongside whom they lived. The author derives his insights both from the latest archaeological and scholarly reports, and from the equally energetic and revealing work of the many groups who seek to find out what Roman life was like by re-enacting it for themselves.

Peter Furtado
General Editor

Opposite:
The pharos or lighthouse at Dubris (Dover) was built in the first century and had a beacon to guide shipping. The church nearby was built byt the Anglo-Saxons, and both are within the grounds of Dover Castle, which remained important militarily until 1945.

INTRODUCTION

BRITAIN WAS PART OF the Roman empire for over 350 years, between AD 43 when the Romans first arrived permanently, and 410 when they finally left. What difference did being part of the Roman empire for so long make to life in Britain? Was the arrival of the Romans a turning-point as significant as, say, the arrival of the Normans in 1066? Or was their presence just a blip in British history, as some have claimed? There have been many assumptions about life in Roman Britain. This book looks at life in Roman Britain not from the point of view of the legionaries posted to the frontier, or the elite in their fine villas, but for an ordinary British family such as lived and worked in one of the many new Roman towns.

Who were the Romans, exactly? Were they all from central Italy, or did they come from all over Europe and North Africa? Why did they come in the first place? Did they want Britain for its riches, or was the invasion part of the politics of empire, or even a campaign strategy? Writing in about AD 98, Tacitus justified the conquest by saying that as well as being 'tolerant of crops and prolific of cattle ... Britain produces gold and silver and other metals, conquest is worthwhile. Their sea also produces pearls.' The addition of Britain to the empire was a political achievement for the Emperor Claudius who marched triumphantly into the important British town of Camulodunum (Colchester) on an elephant. He also assumed the title Britannicus which meant 'Conqueror of Britain'. But the first Roman to invade Britain did so a hundred years earlier as part of his campaign to add Gaul to the empire. In 55 and 54 BC Julius Caesar had brought two military expeditions to Britain. His objective was to stop the Britons helping the Gallic tribes who were still resisting his conquest.

The name Britain came from a first-century BC Greek historian Diodorus Siculus, who called the mainland of the British Isles, Prettanike. By the time Julius Caesar invaded this had become Britannia and its inhabitants, Britons. The Britons themselves probably

Opposite: Hunting deity with a dog; a mixture of a British hunter-god, the Roman god Apollo, and an eastern saviour-god. The worship of deities from Asia and Egypt was introduced to the west under the Roman Empire, and amalgamated with British gods.

The Newport arch, Lincoln, the north gate of the Roman town of Lindum.

called it Alba which meant 'the land' in their own language. They spoke a language called Brythonic, which was similar to Welsh.

The 370 years for which Britain was part of the Roman Empire is a length of time equivalent to that from the English Civil Wars to the present day. During this more recent period of time, a great deal of importance happened: Britain had an agricultural and then an industrial revolution; it gained and lost its own empire; it fought on the winning side in two world wars.

By comparison, how much did Britain change while it was part of the Roman Empire? When people ask what the Romans ever did for us, the answer usually involves roads. The Romans made an immediate and enduring impact on Britain by building eight-thousand miles of roads within the first sixty years they were here.

Second-century Roman oil lamp in the shape of a foot, which was found in London.

Britain had come under a degree of Roman influence even before the legions arrived. When Caesar's troops charged ashore there was already evidence of trade with other parts of the Roman empire. Pre-Roman Britain already had an Iron-Age culture, and at least in activities like metal-working the level of skill was equivalent to that of the Romans. Did the invaders bring technological change?

Once they were here to stay, were the Romans merely occupiers, raking off the profits of the province while holding it down by force? Or did they become integrated into society in Britain?

How much of the British Isles was actually conquered? When the Romans first arrived they subdued the south-east: the border of the original province stretched from Exeter in the south-west to Lincoln in the east. The northern and western parts of mainland Britain remained unconquered. But, by the end of the first century, they had added Wales, the Midlands and the north of England to the province. Roman Britain extended north as far as a line between the Tyne and the Solway Firth. The Romans made several expeditions into Scotland and even advanced the border up to a line between the Clyde and the Firth of Forth for about forty years; then they withdrew to the Tyne and the Solway Firth border. They never went to Ireland.

Map of Britannia at its greatest extent c. AD 122–45.

The society and economy of pre-Roman Britain had been almost entirely rural. In contrast, the Roman empire was urban in orientation, even though the majority of the population of Britannia (as the Romans named their province) still lived in the country. So did all the remarkable aspects of Roman lifestyle, the bath-houses, the forums, the games, pass ordinary Britons by?

Accounts of life in Roman Britain often focus on features like hypocausts and fine dining, enjoyed by the rich inhabitants of the many villas that have been discovered across Britain. But did ordinary Britons enjoy under-floor heating and fine food? How much smaller and less comfortable were their homes?

Metal vessels
from Roman
London.

Opposite top:
An archaeologist
examines pottery
fragments found
at Silchester.

Opposite bottom:
Hadrian's Wall,
the greatest
remaining feature
of Roman Britain.

Did the Romans make any difference to the diet of ordinary people? Which British food was a delicacy enjoyed in Rome? We can now compare the diet of the inhabitants of the province with those of elsewhere in the empire. Did being part of the empire have any impact on religious beliefs and practices in Britain?

The Romans brought their exotic forms of entertainment to Britain, but was everyone lounging in the baths and watching gladiators or was the province too cold and remote for gladiator-fights and chariot racing? The Romans were literate — but what about the Britons under the Roman Empire? Could they read and write? How did the Romans cope with hygiene and disease? All these questions are answered in the pages that follow.

How do we know about life in Roman Britain? What evidence can we trust? Is it written in books or letters which we know have survived from that period? How much physical evidence is there? Can we see signs of Roman Britain from the air? Are discoveries still being made?

There is a great deal of evidence of life in Roman Britain; much has remained buried for years. As archaeologists dig down, they can even discover distinctive moments in the history of Roman Britain, such as the time when three new towns, Londinium, Camulodunum and Verulamium, were burnt to the ground in AD 60 by Boudica, rebellious queen of the Iceni tribe.

As well as architectural features, archaeologists most often dig up fragments of pottery. These can be identified as parts of broken vessels for storing, preparing and eating food. They also tell us that people lived on that site and give us clues as to when they did so. Fragments of bone can be analysed to tell us about both the health and identity of their original owners, animal and human. We can assemble a picture of what people ate and drank in Roman Britain from seeds and pieces of food-processing equipment such as mixing bowls. Seeds are virtually indestructible. Even after they have been burnt, their carbonised remains still reveal what they once were. Their depth in the ground tells us how old they are. Modern techniques such as carbon dating and DNA analysis provide additional information. We can tell where in the Roman Empire the people whose remains are found in Britain originally came from. All this can build up into a picture of who the Britons were and how they lived.

Arbeia gatehouse, the reconstructed entrance to a fort that guarded the River Tyne.

Recent discoveries such as the Vindolanda tablets, fragile letters written in ink on slivers of wood by soldiers manning Hadrian's Wall, tell us a great deal about life in Roman Britain. They even tell us about the socks that shivering soldiers serving on the northern frontier needed to keep themselves warm. They tell us what their commanding officer would serve his dinner guests. Indeed, the greatest remaining feature of Roman Britain is the frontier barrier of Hadrian's Wall itself.

Life in Roman Britain was indeed very different to life in Iron Age Britain, at least for those who lived in the new towns or had dealings with the Roman Empire, through trade or involvement with the military. While it lasted, Britain benefited from being part of the Roman Empire. After it fell and its trading network collapsed, Britain, like the rest of Europe went back to life in a subsistence economy, unable to support the urban middle class which the Romans had created. But many of the things which the Romans had introduced remained, such as their roads, agricultural produce, techniques such as brick-making and literacy. The Latin language, too, survived through its use by the church and as the language of the educated such as priests and lawyers.

In the pages that follow, we find out, what the Romans did for our ancestors, and for us.

FAMILY LIFE

BY THE MID-FIRST CENTURY AD, Rome was far more than a central Italian city-state. Through a series of alliances, wars and diplomatic manoeuvres, Rome already had a huge empire. Its provinces stretched from Pontus and Cappadocia (modern Turkey) in the east to Hispania (Spain) in the west. In the south it included North Africa and in the north, all of Europe as far as the Rhine and the Danube. The 'Romans' themselves were a melting-pot of different races, stirred by trade and war. Even people from far-flung provinces could rise in Roman society. One of the most successful

For ordinary families the household shrine was just a niche in the wall.

Graffiti on the base of a beaker, accompanying a late Roman burial in Winchester.

governors of Britain in the first century of Roman rule, Gnaeus Julius Agricola, was born in southern France. One of the commanders of the garrison at Vindolanda, Flavius Cerialis, was from Batavia (the Netherlands). Even an emperor himself could come from the provinces: Septimius Severus was an African; Hadrian was from Spain.

The Romans conscripted conquered people from across the empire to serve in their army as auxiliaries (non-citizen soldiers, unlike the soldiers in the legions who had to be Roman citizens). They pacified provinces by making their most aggressive inhabitants join their army, then sent them elsewhere. The soldiers who served in the frontier forts were auxiliaries from other provinces: the fort at Vindolanda, near Hadrian's Wall, was manned by Tungrians from modern Belgium and Holland; the Sarmatian cavalry stationed in Britain came from Hungary. Cut off from their own backgrounds, these men soon found that the only familiar ways were Roman ones, and they became an important means of spreading the Roman way of life. So too were legionary soldiers, who on retirement were given land in the provinces where they might settle down and raise families of Roman citizens.

Re-enactors (from the Ermine Street Guard) as auxiliaries. The Romans conscripted provincials with useful skills as cavalry and archers.

After the soldiers, traders were the next to arrive. Londinium (Roman London) grew quickly due to the influx of eager merchants. It began as a river port at the first easy bridging place over the Thames. The first settlers arrived there about AD 50; just ten years later Londinium was the largest town in the province. The historian Tacitus remarked that, as early as AD 60, Londinium was 'famed for commerce and crowded with traders'. The families of immigrants, like the soldiers, lived a Roman lifestyle.

Before the Romans arrived, there were very few towns or even large settlements. The population lived in local communities which the Romans identified as tribes. Neighbouring tribes such as the Catuvellauni and the Trinobantes (both in modern eastern England) seldom co-operated and were frequently hostile to each other. Consequently the tribesmen did not travel far but married other members of their local village or group. They supported themselves by farming and defended themselves against rivals or aggressive neighbours.

The wealthier Britons could thrive under Roman rule. Former tribal leaders became part of an elite layer of society which consisted of soldiers, administrators and landowners. The Romans allowed British tribes who accepted Roman rule to govern themselves. For example, the Atrebates, a southern tribe, had been allies of the Romans even before they invaded, and used imported Roman goods. Members of their elite could enjoy the Roman lifestyle in towns and military centres. Togidubnus, a first-century leader of the Atrebates, was even given authority over other tribes in his area; his villa at Fishbourne near Chichester was palatial in scale.

The arrival of the Romans stimulated existing settlements and the growth of completely new towns, such as Pontes (Staines). The vast majority of Britons continued to live in their rural communities but the towns attracted craftsmen such as workers in metal, textiles, leather and pottery, as Britain became part of an international trading network. Former tribal centres like Calleva Atrebatum (Silchester, now in Hampshire between Reading and Basingstoke) became the hubs of this network. Their markets attracted local farmers who wished to sell their produce. Those that prospered became a middle class between the elite and the majority of Britons. Immigrant traders arrived as well, bringing the Romans' favourite foods and exporting local produce.

Facial reconstruction of a woman whose remains were found in London. She was buried in a fine sarcophagus (stone coffin) with beautiful ornaments. She was probably born in Spain and died aged about 25.

At first, the daily life of farmers in the countryside would not have changed very much. In the towns and military centres, though, people were more likely to adopt a Roman style of life.

Slavery had existed in pre-Roman Britain, when prisoners of war became the property of their captors and criminals lost their freedom. Under the Romans slavery was even more a fact of life. In Italy the economy was completely dependent on slaves but in Britain the institution was less prevalent, though ordinary people might own a slave. One of the commanders of the Vindolanda frontier fort, Flavius Cerialis, owned at least two. The children of slaves were themselves slaves. Their owner could choose to set a slave free by manumission, the process of getting a legal certificate and paying tax according to the slave's value. The slave then became a freedman; his or her former master became their patron. The freed slave changed his or her name to include the names of their former owner.

For most people, slave or free, the working day began at dawn. The family got up and had an informal meal or a drink of water and some bread. In a town, a blacksmith worked most of the hours of daylight. His work involved manual labour, buying and selling, and supervising any slaves and servants he had. Occasionally, perhaps once a week, he might take a break around midday to go to the baths where as well as bathing, he might meet friends and make business

Sculpture of four mother goddesses. Two hold fruit, one has a dog in her lap, and a fourth nurses a baby.

contacts. Women might become involved in their husband's trade or shop. Women were also responsible for looking after children under the age of seven. Older boys might receive some education, help their fathers in their work or begin to learn a trade. Girls would help their mother or learn to weave. Women and slaves did the cleaning, washing, cooking and weaving. In towns, they could buy food or household necessities such as fuel for heating and cooking, or oil for lamps. Shopping in town was a new experience in Roman Britain. At the main meal of the day, in the early evening, the family ate together. The children ate sitting up but if their parents had adopted Roman habits the adults might recline on couches. After the meal everyone went to bed.

Religion was a key part of Roman-style family life. The father honoured hearth and home at the household shrine. There was a strong element of ancestor worship because the spirits of the dead (*manes*) were supposed to be protective towards family members. The father said prayers and made offerings to the *Genus Familiaris* or guardian spirit of the household. The household shrine, or *lararium*, was a cupboard or niche in the house which contained a figure of the *Genus Familiaris*, with a toga over his head to avoid seeing or hearing any ill-omens. The *lararium* also held a *patera* or sacrificial dish, and a napkin. In addition there might have been figures representing other gods such as Mars, the god of war; Bacchus, the god of wine or Venus Lucinus, the goddess of childbirth.

The Romans introduced their distinctive system for naming children. The day a baby was named was very important to the Romans. Girls were named eight days after they were born, boys nine days after they were born. Free-born Roman males were given three names. The first name, or *praenomen*, was their personal name. The second name, or *nomen,* was the name of their *gens* or clan. The third name, or *cognomen*, was the name of their branch of the family. This name might have begun as a nickname such as Caesar (which meant 'hairy'). Women had two names: their personal name and the name of their clan.

Roman portable shrine made from lead, depicting the goddess Minerva, wearing a helmet, with a shield in her right hand and a spear in her left.

Reconstruction of a Roman cutler's stall at the Museum of London, AD 100. Apart from the bundles of tools at the bottom, they are all Roman finds from London with reconstructed handles.

Britons usually had two names: their personal name and a patronymic (their father's name) such as Marinianus Belcati or Bellaus Bellini. Slaves had only a single name; Privatus was a common slave name.

On a child's naming day, the guests brought metal trinkets called *crepundia* which were strung around the baby's neck. In addition free-born babies were given a *bulla* or locket containing a good-luck charm to be worn around the neck. Children of wealthy parents might have a *bulla* made from gold. A poor child's *bulla* would be made from leather. Mothers cared for their children until they were seven years old. Then the father took responsibility. He might begin to train them

Child's deer-skin shoe showing the leather laces and the holes for stitching the shoe together; from the Boscombe Down Roman coffin, found in Wiltshire in 2007, in which the skeleton of a woman was found cradling a child.

to work in his skill or trade. He might also teach the boys skills like hunting. Alternatively he could arrange for him to be educated. At the age of 12 the sons of Roman citizens such as legionaries were old enough to wear a *toga praetexta* which had a purple border. At the age of 16, they could put on a man's toga, the *toga virilis*, which was plain white. But only Roman citizens were entitled to wear the toga. The majority of Britons only became citizens in AD 212 when an imperial edict made all free-born subjects of the empire Roman citizens. The toga was a long white costume made of wool. It was the traditional Roman dress of a mature man which he wore only on formal occasions. After he received his toga a Roman boy took off his *bulla*. His father then took him to the forum to show off his grown-up clothes. Then they came home and had a party.

At 12 a girl was considered old enough to get married or engaged to be married. A girl kept her *bulla* until her wedding day. Boys could not marry until they were 14, although usually people were older when they got married. Parents often arranged marriages for their children. Arranged marriages often began with a formal betrothal, which was like an engagement or promise to marry at a later date. The bride's family was expected to give her a dowry: money, land or property such as cattle. The wedding ceremony was held at the bride's home. There were special customs such as animal sacrifices and feasts. Marriage made the couple's children legitimate, which meant they had the same rights and status as their parents. For example, if their parents were citizens, they, too, were citizens.

The toga, the formal dress of a mature Roman male. This is a *toga praetexta* (with a crimson border), as worn by young boys, magistrates, some priests and others of high rank or distinction. Ordinary citizens wore a plain white version.

HOME AND
NEIGHBOURHOOD

WHEN THE ROMANS first arrived in Britain their great campaign of construction had an immediate impact on the appearance of the land. Towns began to develop at road junctions and river crossings, such as Durobrivae (Water Newton near Peterborough) and Pontes (Staines) as well as principal tribal settlements such as Venta Belgarum (Winchester). The traditional shape of houses and buildings even began to change, from round to straight-sided. In the countryside the Britons continued to live in their familiar roundhouses but in the new towns the houses and other buildings were now rectangular. The construction techniques for both were timber frames with wattle-and-daub infill. Houses were built on solid foundations of locally available stone or rubble.

In places where Roman influence was strongest all new buildings were rectilinear, and laid out on a rectangular street grid. This originated in the standard plan of a Roman fort or military camp. These were roughly the shape of a playing card with gates in the centre of each side. Main roads ran through the town from gate to gate.

Reconstruction of a traditional round house, at Butser Ancient Farm in Hampshire.

The grid of streets created blocks in which shops and workshops developed, especially along the main roads where they attracted passing trade. The streets of major towns like Verulamium (St Albans) were lined by workshops and shops producing metalwork, pottery, glass, furniture, leather goods, shoes, clothing and textiles. In addition, they offered decorative objects such as enamelling, bone-working and mosaic. There were also consumer services such as barbers and laundries. The individual shops were typically nine metres wide and thirty-one metres deep. They were built as a continuous terrace with living accommodation behind or above them.

Above:
Plan of a workshop with living quarters.

Above left:
Work such as drying and curing hides took place around the walls of a roundhouse.

Left: The smoky atmosphere of a roundhouse with a chalk floor.

21

An internal wall showing traditional wattle-and-daub infill.

Places which had been the principal tribal settlements before the Romans became the administrative centres for the surrounding areas (*civitates*). Main roads ran straight through them; for example the road from Londinium (London) to the fort of Isca Silurum (Caerleon) ran along the main street of the pre-existing settlement Calleva Atrebatum (Silchester). Forts with small garrisons of auxiliary soldiers were placed at strategic junctions and river crossings. Settlements grew up around forts like Bremetenacum Veteranorum (Ribchester, Lancashire). Such a settlement was known as a *vicus*, a rural settlement or area was a *pagus*.

At the centre of the town was the forum which was placed centrally like the headquarters of a military camp. In towns which began as military centres, such as Camulodunum (Colchester) and Glevum (Gloucester), the forum was built over the site of the former headquarters of the legionary fortress. The forum was both a legal and a commercial centre. Three sides of the forum had colonnades or covered walkways supported by columns. A basilica comprised the fourth side. This was a large, high building with a central vaulted space or nave with aisles on either side. It was used as a law court and for meetings of the town council. The open space outside was used as a market and for public meetings, announcements and posting public notices. In other parts of the Roman empire there were usually temples in the open space of the forum, but this was very rare in Britain. The colonnades could be used for stalls and shops, such as an oyster bar or a fishmonger.

An ordinary family would have lived in accommodation, perhaps just a single room, above or behind a shop or workshop. The building

The high-quality finish of the mosaics at the site of the former County Hospital in Dorchester is exceptional for the region.

would have been part of a row or terrace, sometimes with a roofed colonnade in front. In Verulamium, examples of these have been discovered in blocks of four. The front of the shop was open to the street, with wooden shutters so it could be closed at night. Some shops set up counters or tables in the colonnade itself. Like the forum, the colonnade was formed of wooden columns supporting a sloping, tiled roof. The footpath of a colonnade on a main street might have been trampled earth but in a forum it was paved with stone. The craftsman probably rented from the owner of the building who might well have been a leading member of the local tribe, who perhaps paid to have the block built with a loan from an immigrant money-lender. In the early Roman period the building was probably timber framed with wattle-and-daub walls and a slate or thatched roof. Later buildings of the same type were built with stone, rubble and tiles. Roman influence brought about the increasing

Reconstruction of a blacksmith's shop.

use of stone, at first for the foundations. The Romans preferred oak for their structural timbers such as the corner posts and the horizontal beams. The walls might have been finished in plaster. More expensive buildings might have had frescoed paintings on the walls, but in modest houses the walls were probably plain.

Most families cooked, ate and slept in a single room. In cold weather, it was heated by an open-topped brazier of burning coals. The family used the public baths to bathe and a pot or latrine bucket for other needs which they would have emptied outside. Rows of shops and workshops built later sometimes had more rooms at the back, with some of them sub-divided by internal walls made from clay and plaster applied to light frames formed by hurdle-work made from withies. Such buildings had wooden floors and back doors with access to yards. A gravel path led to a gate which opened onto a back or side street. In towns water had to be brought from nearby wells or streams. If a family prospered they might move to a larger townhouse (*domus*) with room for dependants such as servants and slaves.

For the majority who lived in the country, change was more gradual. The traditional British roundhouses had two entrances opposite each other. The fireplace was central, and probably fitted with iron fire dogs and with a pot hanging over it. The smoke escaped by seeping through the thatch, so the interior could become quite smoky depending on atmospheric conditions. When entering, a guest

23

Roman key, from Cambourne, Cambridgeshire.

moved to the left around the periphery of the hut. Work activities such as the preparation of hides and weaving took place next to the outside walls. As in townhouses, the occupants would have slept on the floor or on low beds like wooden platforms. Clothes and other items were kept in wooden chests or on shelves around the walls. Water had to be brought from nearby streams. Food supplies might have come from communal storage facilities such as underground meat stores or a wooden granary. Villages and settlements might have a communal latrine, which was a hole in the ground over which a shelter and a seat had been built. Wood ash from the fire in the house was collected and used to deodorise the contents of the hole.

Merchants and traders from elsewhere in the empire were among the first to explore the possibilities of Britannia. Traders followed the army into new provinces of the Roman empire. Traders' activities included lending money to locals who wished to build on their land in the developing towns. One of them, Titus Tammonius Victor, left a tombstone in memory of his wife, Flavia Victorina. There were so many immigrant traders in a town like Calleva Atrebatum that they formed a guild of foreigners and dedicated a plaque at a small temple in the town. Successful foreign traders like Titus Tammonius Victor might be rich enough to live in a larger townhouse in the Roman style. These larger townhouses were built in the less densely populated parts of town, away from the centre. Members of the town council were also rich enough to belong to the minority who could afford one of these townhouses.

Townhouses were built on the corridor plan. This had either a colonnade or a corridor which ran along the front with rooms ranged

Reconstruction of the site of the Roman settlement at Dorchester, Dorset.

behind it. The house could be extended by a second wing, making an L-shaped plan. Walls and possibly a porch separated the dwelling from the street and enclosed a forecourt. This could be laid out as a garden.

The reception and living-rooms were entered from the colonnade or corridor and included a *tablinum* and a *triclinium*. The *tablinum* was where the householder received guests and did business. The *triclinium* was the formal dining room. Service rooms such as the kitchen were placed at the end. The bedrooms were on the upper floor. Some town dwellers had a smallholding (*hortus*) outside the town. The aspiration of many town dwellers was to enjoy their own rustic villa. Members of the elite sometimes built a rustic villa on their *hortus* and expanded it into a farm.

The basic rustic villa in Britannia was a single-storey building built on the corridor plan similar to the townhouse. Again the foundations and lower walls were built of stone; the upper walls were timber framed with wattle-and-daub infill. The roof was pitched with either clay or slate tiles. The main rooms were placed behind the corridor with the principal reception room in the centre and the kitchen and private rooms placed on either side. If the farm was successful enough the owners could add wings projecting forwards on either side to form a courtyard at the front. The wings contained farmyard facilities such as stables, storerooms, grain-drying ovens and granaries as well as servants' quarters and bath-houses.

Aerial view of Silchester showing the street grid, forum and amphitheatre.

Overleaf:
A Romano-British family lived in a single-roomed house with small, high windows. Cooking was done on an open brazier and the family ate sitting up – unlike the wealthy Romans who preferred to recline whilst they ate.

WORK

MOST PEOPLE WORKED on farms. The Britons' agriculture had been a mixture of growing grain and raising livestock: wheat, barley, oats with horses, cattle, pigs, sheep and goats. The Romans, however, introduced their preferred forms of grain, fruit, herbs, vegetables and animals. Some of these, like the olive, would not grow in Britain but those that did became permanent additions.

As part of the Romans' great trade network, surplus produce could now be sold for profit, and communities which had only produced enough to feed themselves before could produce far more, and take the extra to the nearest town to sell. A Roman garrison was itself a large market. But by the fourth century, grain from Britain was being exported to Germany. By that time many of the farms had changed from small settlements to larger estates, sometimes around a Roman-style villa.

A traditional stone quern for grinding grain into flour. It required a quarter turn, back and forth.

The army, up to 55,000 men, had to be supplied with wheat, barley and meat. Life in farming communities began to change to meet the demand. The Romans took some of the harvest as a grain tax. They also helped to increase yields by introducing new techniques and equipment. These included crop rotation in the form of a winter-spring crop sequence of oats, followed by wheat and finally beans. The fields had to be cleaned, dug and ploughed. They were fertilised by spreading them with manure or marl clay to prepare the soil for planting. The old wooden ploughs were replaced by ones with iron edges, though still drawn by oxen. The most common types of wheat, emmer and spelt, grew much taller than modern wheat. Emmer and spelt grew to about two metres high, and could be damaged by being blown over or becoming saturated. When the grain was ripe, it was cut with sickles or two-handed scythes. It took a single man one and a half days to harvest a *jugerum* of wheat (a *jugerum* was 240 by 120 feet of land). The stalks were cut for straw, its length depending on what it was wanted for. Long stalks were needed for thatching; shorter lengths were suitable for fodder during the winter or litter in stables and byres (cowsheds), or were burnt in the fields for fertiliser.

Grain had to be threshed to separate the edible part from the husk or straw. It was spread over a paved floor, then horses or mules were driven over it or a threshing sledge was dragged over it. This was a block of wood weighted with stones and nails underneath it. Then the remaining part had to be winnowed to separate the grain from the husk or chaff. The simplest way to do this was to toss it in the air so that the lighter chaff blew away. After winnowing, the grain remained enclosed in an inedible spikelet. Emmer and spelt needed to be parched (heated and pounded) to release the grain. During the Roman period, a newer variety, bread wheat, became popular. This did not need to be parched. Grain could be stored for long periods, after it had been dried. The Romans incorporated drying kilns into the granaries where the grain was kept. These incorporated a variation of the hypocaust.

Finally the grain had to be ground into flour. In rural communities this was done at home using stone mills known as querns. The grain was ground between two

Samian ware vase found in London.

Roof tiles.

A jar used to keep salt, one of Roman Britain's biggest exports.

circular stones, turned by hand. A long handle fitted into the upper stone and was given a quarter turn back and forth. The grain might have to be ground several times to get a fine enough flour. The Romans introduced bigger, hour-glass-shaped, rotary querns which were used in towns and at military establishments. These could be turned by a donkey harnessed to the mill.

By the third century, on large estates, the balance had changed from grain to sheep farming. As wool became a more profitable product for export than grain, sheep farming became the bigger activity. The common breeds, such as the soay, produced plenty of wool which only had to be collected because they shed it naturally, rather than having to be sheared – although shearing produced a better fleece. The soay's coarse wool was suitable for rugs, capes and mattresses. The Romans introduced improved breeds of sheep which produced finer wool which could be made into softer cloth. This became a speciality export of the province, one praised by Roman writers.

The area for a mile or two around a town or fort was also cultivated for cereals and vegetables. The outlying fields and woods produced wheat, barley and oats. There were byres (cowsheds) within the towns themselves. Pigs grazed in the surrounding woodland, which also produced timber and firewood. As well as draft animals, livestock produced horn, hides, meat, lard, milk and cheese. Before the Romans, the Britons preferred to eat mutton and goat but beef and pork were very much part of the Roman way of life and the army's rations. A new market for beef and pork developed. The Romans also introduced greater diversity: farmed animals such as rabbits and domestic fowl such as geese; grape vines and orchard crops such as apples, medlars, cherries and plums and vegetables such as asparagus, beetroot, cabbage, carrot and celery. Around Silchester blackberries, elderberries, mulberries, walnuts and herbs such as coriander, dill, fennel, chervil and parsley were picked.

The Romans had first come to Britain under the impression that the country was rich in minerals. Metal was vital for the empire's coin supply, armaments and equipment in addition to its many uses in daily life. Mines came under military control because the emperor claimed all metal. It always received a military escort when it was transported, and it was always melted down and re-used.

There were mines with silver-rich lead ore at Charterhouse in the Mendips, the Peak District, the Pennines and in Wales; tin and other ores from Cornwall; iron ore from the Forest of Dean and the east Midlands. There was only one gold mine, in south Wales at Dolaucothi (Pumsaint, Carmarthenshire). In Roman Britain small-scale working was normal, but the lead-mining at Charterhouse was conducted on an exceptional scale. At first, the lead was mined by soldiers from the Second Augusta legion, but by Vespasian's reign (AD 69–79) the work had been subcontracted to private companies.

Most mines were worked opencast. The ore was cut with hammer and chisel, then gathered into baskets with wide-mouthed oak shovels. Working in the mines was used as a punishment; one miner in eight died each year. Because of this, miners were slaves, prisoners of war or criminals. It was worse for gold-miners, who worked underground. They often died of lung diseases from the dust as well as having to avoid rockfalls and shaft collapses.

Until the third century, tin from Cornwall was not worth mining because tin from Spain was cheaper, but thereafter the trade routes were so disrupted that it became worth extracting. It was also needed to make alloys such as bronze (copper and tin) and pewter (tin and lead).

Coal was used for drying grain and smelting lead as well as for heating and cooking. There were over two hundred coal-extraction sites in Roman Britain: in Durham, Yorkshire, Nottinghamshire, Derbyshire, the Forest of Dean, south Wales and Somerset. It was transported in ships and carts.

Metalwork, enamelling, pottery, glassware, bone-working, carpentry, leather goods, shoes, clothing and textiles were mostly produced in small workshops. Metalwork was mostly wrought iron made by smiths. Some individuals knew how to make steel by adding carbon to the process, but because steel shatters on stone, the Romans chose to make softer iron blades which could be resharpened.

First-century bronze bell.

Blacksmiths made tools and implements from lengths of iron known as blooms. These were heated until they were in a red-hot, semi-solid state, then cut, beaten and welded into shape with shears, hammer and tongs. The finished products were agricultural implements, kitchen equipment, chains, or wheel rims. The Romans also knew how to work lead to make pipes.

Textile workers also worked as individual craftsmen. The wool trade produced characteristic garments such as the hooded cloak known as the *byrrus Britannicus*. As the production of wool grew increasingly profitable, in certain places, production became more concentrated. Corinium (Cirencester) became a centre of the woollen industry which produced goods such as mattresses, rugs or draperies. Mattresses were a sack of wool or linen stuffed with wool. There were further exceptions to the pattern of small workshops: weaving shops proliferated on the big estates around Venta Icenorum (Caistor by Norwich) and Venta Belgarum (Winchester). Other types of workshop, such as fulleries, developed alongside them. These acted as laundries as well as for finishing the cloth-making process. Newly woven cloth had to be shrunk and bleached and soiled garments were brought in for cleaning or renovation. New cloth was dyed and old garments redyed.

Blown green glass flagon, second century, found in Aberdeenshire.

During the second half of the first century there was a surge in imports to supply the Romans, including many household items such as bowls and plates. Top of the range were the red-brown glazed dishes from Gaul, known as Samian ware. But the Romans found local sources of supply. Native potters began to supply the needs of their fellow Britons from their own workshops. All less-valuable items

The maker's stamp from the base of a Samian ware bowl, found in Dorchester, Dorset.

made from clay, such as roof tiles, bricks, storage jars and kitchenware were home-produced. The Romans also introduced brickmaking to Britain. Roman bricks were flatter than modern bricks, and were often used as *pilae* which supported hypocausts underfloor heating systems. The characteristic Roman roof tiles, or pantiles, were formed from two pieces: the flat *tegula* which had flat ridges on both ends and the curved *imbrex* which bridged the gap. Hollow bricks were made to allow hot air from underfloor heating systems to pass upwards through walls.

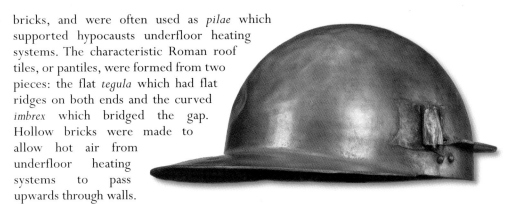

Helmet of a first-century Roman legionary, found in the River Thames, London.

The market for individual potters was usually confined to their local area. Their finished wares were packed into saddlebags or straw, then hawked around on donkey, packhorse or cart until sold. But during the second century, at Durobrivae (Water Newton, Cambridgeshire), more concentrated production of pottery began. Even today around Water Newton, when it floods, pieces of Roman pottery are still washed up. Each pot was thrown by hand but 500–600 pieces at a time were fired in large kilns. They produced coarse grey and buff ware for local markets, and *mortaria* for wider distribution. Their characteristic red or brown light beakers are known as Castor-ware. It was exported all over Europe and even reached beyond the borders of the empire to Germany.

The fish trade was one of the most remarkable examples of the Roman trading network. Fish and shellfish were brought from the coast to inland towns where they became a popular part of the diet of even ordinary people. Oysters became one of Roman Britain's most prestigious exports.

Salt was a vital product for preserving as well as flavouring food. Britain had more saltpans than any other province. Sites such as Salinae (Droitwich, in Worcestershire and Middlewitch, in Cheshire) produced another one of the province's biggest exports.

Broken roof tile, showing front and back pawprints of a small dog, or a fox, which trod on the tile while it was still wet. Dorchester, Dorset.

FOOD AND DRINK

THE ROMANS GREATLY increased the variety of foods available. Most of their favourites, like garlic and onions, could be grown here. The few that could not, like olives, artichokes and figs, were imported. The result was a polarisation between those who followed the Roman tastes and those who stuck to the characteristic diet of the Britons. An immigrant from southern Europe would have liked olive oil and wine; whereas a native Briton probably preferred beer and butter, the latter made from goat's milk.

Food had to be preserved during the winter. This was done by salting, smoking or drying it. Many animals were killed in the autumn because it was difficult to feed them during the winter when they could not graze. The Romans introduced crops like turnips which could be used as winter feed to keep some livestock alive through the winter.

The basic food of both the Romans and the Britons was made from grain. It could be made into anything from bread and cake to porridge. The barley porridge or gruel was known as *pils* or *pulmentus*. Barley also made good griddle cakes, or bannocks, which were cooked on hot stones in the hearth, but bread made from barley flour is flat and heavy due to a lack of gluten. Emmer wheat was only suitable for porridge because it didn't rise, but it could be made into cakes of a doughnut type. Bread made from spelt wheat rose a little, like puffy pitta or nan bread.

The Romans had a hierarchy of breads: *autopyron* was a coarse, dark mixture of bran and flour for slaves and dogs; *athletae* was an unleavened bread mixed with soft curd cheese; *bucellatum* was a biscuit or dried bread for the army; *artophites* was a light leavened bread. White bread was the most prestigious even though Roman medical writers noted that brown was more nutritious. In towns, round loaves of a type of sourdough bread could be bought from bakers who baked them in brick ovens lit by wood or charcoal fires. When the oven was hot enough the ashes were raked out, the bread was put in and the

Roman cookery expert, Sally Grainger, cooking an authentic Roman dish in a clay pot on a gridiron, over a charcoal fire.

mouth closed. As well as bakers, pastry cooks and confectioners sold their wares in towns.

Both olives and olive oil were imported in the characteristic Roman storage vessel, the amphora. It was closed with a cork bung sealed with wax. There were a variety of shapes for different products. The sizes were consistent, too, so the vessel was also a unit of measurement. Most olive oil came from Spain in a distinctive round amphora. Most imported wine came from France in an amphora with a pointed end which could be buried in an earth floor to make it stand upright. The Romans used olive oil for frying and in recipes such as salad dressings. It had many other uses including fuel for lamps.

The Britons used butter for frying. If they had not made cheese before, they certainly did under the Romans for whom it was an important part of the army's rations. The characteristic Roman mixing bowl, the *mortarium*, was particularly suitable for making cheese. It had pieces of grit embedded in its inner surface. These retained the bacteria which curdled the milk so it was not necessary to add rennet. A *mortarium* also had a spout on its rim which allowed the liquid whey to be poured off when the milk separated. The curd cheese which remained could be flavoured with herbs or made into a hard cheese.

Ordinary people in both town and country ate pottage (meat and vegetable stew) or porridge-like dishes, with added herbs and spices. An essential for those who had a taste for Roman cooking was fish sauce.

Second-century Roman relief showing delivery of wine *amphorae*. Their pointed ends were buried in the ground to keep them upright.

For the Romans it was a fifth flavour alongside sweet, sour, savoury and bitter. They used it instead of salt.

There were several varieties of fish sauce. They were made from fermented fish entrails and salt. *Garum* was made from the fresh blood and viscera of selected fish, mainly mackerel. It was added to food by the diner, like a condiment. *Liquamen* was used by cooks. It took up to four months to make. Small fish, often anchovy, were layered with salt in pits. It separated into a paste at the bottom, allec, which was used as a pickle. Above it was the liquor, *liquamen*. *Muria*, a fish brine, formed from the water that leeched out of slices of salted fish. It was paler than *liquamen*, similar to Thai fish sauce. *Muria* was favoured by the lower classes. They used it to make dipping sauces for their bread and dressings for their leaf salads. The simplest salad dressing was *oenogarum*: *garum* mixed with wine. This could be served either hot or cold.

The Britons had been eating dishes like smoky fish stew for centuries. This was made from bacon, leeks and smoked fish and depended on the availability of fish. The Romans made fish much more easily available inland. The Britons could buy cod, ling (a type of cod), haddock, grey mullet, herring, sea bream, crab and lobster in the markets. The fish was preserved in brine to keep it fresh. In the forum a shellfish shop sold periwinkles, mussels, whelks, cockles and scallops. It also sold the delicacy which everyone in Britain ate: oysters. Oysters kept well and were transported long distances. Oysters from Britain were a luxury in Rome itself. In Britain, though, spices like pepper were only available to the wealthy.

Porridge and bread were the basic foods of Roman Britain.

A *mortarium*, the characteristic Roman mixing bowl.

Cooking a soup on a portable iron cooker: Roman soup included many types of greens.

Ordinary people cooked in porous clay pots.

A cabbage salad with a honey and vinegar dressing.

Rosemary, one of the herbs introduced by the Romans.

A copper-alloy, double-ended Roman fork, 140mm long, possibly used for eating shellfish or snails. Dorchester, Dorset.

In towns and military areas, pork and beef were commonly eaten. In rural areas, the Britons were more used to the meat of sheep or goats. A typical urban craftsman family would have a soup or stew such as *tisanam barcoram* for their evening meal. This contained several different types of green vegetables, chickpeas, lentils, bacon, fennel, *muria* and some bacon, mutton, or meat fat. Herbs such as lovage and spices would have been added. Most ordinary people cooked in clay pots over a gridiron in their living-room. Pots and bowls were porous because they were unglazed, so it was necessary to replace them regularly. Iron pans lasted longer but were more expensive. A typical meal was eaten with bread accompanied by beer or well-watered wine. The most expensive ingredients would have been the imported spices, chickpeas and lentils. On special occasions the family might have begun their meal with a cabbage salad with a honey and vinegar dressing.

The Romans added numerous vegetables and salad ingredients to what was already available in Britain. The Britons already had leeks, celery, mushrooms, sorrel and wild greens such as cabbage, watercress, nettles, and penny cress.

As well as onions and garlic the Romans introduced peas, broad beans, carrots, radish, beetroot, ground elder and rape. The carrots they brought were small and white, like early parsnips. Cabbage was the leaf-and-stalk kind like kale or winter greens. For salads they introduced leafy lettuce (like Webb's) and endive. They combined them with wild leaves like (young) stinging nettles and the small nettle which they introduced; and they used the leaves of root vegetables such as beet and turnips.

Other edible plants were introduced but are now out of cultivation, including mallow, orache, and fat hen. The Romans also brought herbs including mint, chervil, alecost, thyme, coriander, rosemary and summer savory.

The Britons already kept domestic fowl such as chickens, ducks and geese, but poultry was a high-status item more often found in towns or on military sites than in the country. They were cooked whole rather than jointed.

Eggs were a distinctive feature of Roman cooking. They were eaten hard-boiled as a first course, dipped in cumin, or baked in hot embers, or used as a binding agent in recipes or to make a *patina*. This could be a sweet or savoury dish, named after the type of pan used to cook it. A savoury *patina* was similar to a modern frittata or a quiche. The sweet varieties were forms of custard with fruit or honey. Some sweet *patina* recipes included fish sauce.

The Romans introduced rabbits as farm animals. The hare was native to Britain but the type of rabbit the Romans introduced came from Spain (they were not hardy enough to survive the winter in the wild, in Britain). Hares were also kept on the farm for food. The Romans also introduced pigeons and doves. They were kept in dovecotes. Snails were another popular introduction.

The Britons already had wild cherries and other wild berries such as gooseberries and blackberries. The Romans introduced the sour cherry, the mulberry and the grape. By using grafting, they encouraged orchard crops such as apples and pears. The only sweeteners were honey and dried fruits such as figs and raisins. (The Romans were aware of sugar but it was so rare it was only used as a medicine.) Dates were imported in carrot-shaped amphorae. Bees were kept in hives or apiaries in rural settlements and around a town or fort. Roman-style sweets and confections, in the form of pastries, became available in towns. They were flavoured with nuts. The Romans added the walnut, sweet chestnut, almond and the stone pine to the native hazel.

A beehive reconstructed in a rural settlement.

Reconstruction of
a small granary

Alcoholic drinks were safer to drink than water which easily became contaminated. Bad water could cause stomach upsets or diarrhoea. Milk did not keep for long. Beer was half the price of wine. It was a type of ale, made from wheat. The way in which it was brewed produced a strong drink from the initial fermentation and a weaker brew from the leftovers (wort). Beer was drunk at all levels of society. Ordinary people drank beer in ceramic beakers. The Britons used honey to make mead. This was a strong alcoholic drink made from honey and water. These are self-fermenting when combined. Mead could be flavoured by adding other ingredients such as wheat, fruit or spices.

Wine was mainly imported from France because it was nearest; but vintage wines such as Falernian and sweet wines from Cos and Rhodes were also imported. There were markets for good wines in towns like Camulodunum and Londinium. The Romans drank their wine mixed with water. Drinking it neat was regarded as barbaric and even dangerous. Consequently they used sets of jugs and bowls to mix their wine. The rich often served their wine in elaborate wine sets made from silver. Ordinary people used ceramic jugs and cups.

They also drank wine mixed with spices or sweetened with honey (*mulsum*). Wine vinegar from flat wine was made. Known as sour or ordinary wine (*acetum*), it was added to water to ensure that it was safe to drink. The mixture was known as *posca*. They made sweetened wines by adding honey after the wine had been boiled down to a third of its volume.

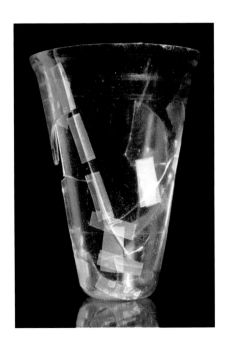

Above: This delicate little fourth-century Roman glass beaker was discovered at Boscombe Down, Wiltshire.

Left: Olive oil, imported from Spain, came in distinctively shaped, round amphorae.

Shopping and Style

THE ROMAN EMPIRE was a vast market economy with a single currency and a well-established system of weights and measures. South-eastern Britain had been developing its own economy for at least one hundred years before the Romans arrived, but there had been different types of coins in circulation and varying weights and measures. Belgic tribes like the Atrebates issued their own coins, but there were also coins from Armorica, in Gaul, and even from Greece, in circulation. People had to work out the value of different coins according to how much silver or gold they contained. As well as coins people used metal bars or salt to buy goods. As well as haggling over the price, they had to negotiate what their units of value were worth. Even in these pre-Roman years, pottery was imported from Armorica and wine from Italy while metal was exported. This was probably why the Romans gained the impression that Britain was 'rich in metals'.

The Romans brought their own currency. The basic unit was the *denarius*, from which we derive the old abbreviation 'd' for a penny. A Roman legionary was paid 300 silver *denarii* a year. Like a modern pound or euro, a *denarius* could be subdivided into numerous coins of less value. One *denarius* was worth four bronze *sesterces*. A *sestertius* was worth four copper *as*. An *as* was worth four *quadrans*. The most valuable coin was the gold *aureus* which was worth twenty-five *denari* or one hundred *sesterces*.

A uniform system of weights and measures was equally important. The Roman basic unit of weight was the *libra* (pound); about 327 grammes. Items like bars of metal had their weight stamped onto them. The *libra* was divided into twelve *unicae* or ounces (about 27 grammes each). Scales were used for measuring small amounts. Larger amounts of liquid or dry goods, such as grain, were measured by the *modius*. This was a standardised container with a flat rim, usually made of bronze, which held about 8.6 litres. The *sextarius* was one sixteenth of a *modius*; about half a litre or a pint and a quarter. Grain

Opposite: Reconstruction of the Roman town of Letocetum, Staffordshire, as it might have looked in the second century. Artwork by Ivan Lapper.

Basketry hat,
from the Roman
site at Newstead,
Melrose.

merchants checked that a *modius* contained full measure by running a rule over the top. Full measure was level with the top. At Vindolanda, a *modius* of barley cost two *sesterces* and one *as*. Street vendors and shopkeepers used the type of balance nowadays called a steelyard: a portable and versatile device which could weigh a wide range of produce. Made from copper alloy, it was a beam hung from a pivot with a sliding counterweight at one end. The goods were hung from a hook at the other end of the beam. The weight of the goods was calculated by that of the counterweight multiplied by its distance from the pivot. Steelyards several feet long were used to weigh sacks of flour and other commodities.

The towns provided markets for both large and small-scale transactions. Individuals made their purchases from the stalls and shopfronts along the main streets. Merchants, corporations and officials conducted larger transactions in the forum where money changers offered their services. Other transactions included paying taxes like the grain tax, loans, deals regarding imports and exports and supplying the military.

A hoard of third-
century Roman
coins, found at
Falkirk.

The roads allowed itinerant salesmen to carry goods such as pottery or tools on pack animals or carts to rural settlements, possibly also acting as middlemen taking produce such as fruit, vegetables or woollens back into town for retailers to sell.

Shopping for food was an everyday task because most foodstuffs did not keep unless they had been dried or salted, like bacon. There were specialist shops like greengrocers and fishmongers, as well as fast food outlets among the shops and stalls in the colonnades and in the forum. Bakers and confectioners sold rolls and pastries. Other stalls offered fare like chickpea pancakes. Itinerant foodsellers sold cakes and sausages from trays. Butchers were eager to provide their customers with choice cuts of meat or game. One bas-relief carving shows a butcher, standing, jointing a side of bacon while his wife sits, writing on a tablet. Ordinary families were unlikely to be able to afford jewellery but the Britons had a taste for brooches which were useful for securing cloaks, leaving both hands free. Objects like mirrors were also rare: they were made from polished bronze. Ordinary people probably only ever saw their reflections in water. Beakers for drinking water or beer were essential for the households of ordinary Britons rather than the wine sets which the elite used. Richer women shopped for finer materials than those woven in their own households, such as silk or cotton. Ordinary Britons wore homespun but they kept their taste for pins and brooches, which were practical as well as an adornment.

Illustration of a steelyard for weighing goods.

Adornments of local semi-precious stones like amber were less expensive than those of silver or gold. Pins, bracelets and rings were sometimes made from jet, a form of lignite which can be polished until it becomes shiny. It was thought to have magical power because it attracts static electricity after it has been rubbed. It could make the hairs of your arm stand up as well as giving you a tingling sensation if it was touched. Rings and bracelets were worn as a charm, talisman or emblem of rank. Signet rings served as proof of identity and were used to seal legal documents such as wills.

Bronze and silver pins.

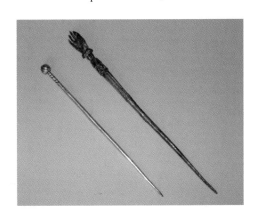

A visit to the bath-house, with its hot and cold rooms, and areas for relaxing and for massage, was a part of the Roman

A Roman-style loom.

lifestyle which most people in towns would have appreciated. The rich went every day; for ordinary people, once a week was more likely. A few women could afford the additional extravagance of using the baths as beauty salons where they could have their hair done. Roman women used face cream to whiten their skin. Elsewhere in the empire this was made from refined animal fat, starch and lead, but in Britain tin was used instead of lead.

Taverns served wine, beer and *posca* with snacks such as olives or bread and a dipping sauce. They also attracted gambling and prostitutes. Hot take-away food was also available at stalls that served their dishes from removable bowls fitted into the counter top.

Clothing was another aspect of lifestyle in which there was a polarisation between the Romans and the Britons. As southern Europeans, the Romans preferred to have bare legs whereas the Britons wore leggings (*bracae*) like other northerners. If necessary, for hunting or fieldwork, the Romans protected their legs with wrappings or puttees bound with wool. Most clothing was woven from wool. The basic item of Roman

Wool dyed in bright colours.

Roman sandals
(*caligae*).

dress was the tunic (*tunica*). This was like a big T-shirt, made from two
pieces of fabric sewn together. Men's tunics had elbow-length sleeves
and covered the body to below the knees. They were worn with a belt
or girdle so they could be pulled up in front for hunting or manual
work. They were usually dyed; both the Romans and the Britons liked
bright colours. The Britons had been capable of dying their wool in
surprisingly bright colours even before the Romans came. In addition
to blue, red, sea-green, saffron yellow, and purple shades were
available. The Britons wove or dyed their woollens with colours made
from ingredients like woad or ochre. They could make patterns,
including check. They also liked embroidery and ornamental fringes.

During the day, if necessary, people wore more than one tunic.
The tunic nearest the body (*subucula*) functioned as underwear.
Manual labourers' tunics were sleeveless. Children's tunics
had long sleeves. Boys' tunics had stripes down the sides
as did those of upper-class men.

Britons wore tunics which were similar in
length, with sleeves. The main difference was
bracae or ankle-length trousers worn under the
tunics. At first, the Romans despised both the
bracae and *feminalia* (riding breeches worn
with leg wrappings). But, as auxiliary
soldiers from northern Europe formed a
substantial part of the garrison, attitudes
became more relaxed. Only citizens were
entitled to wear the toga. The majority of

A drawing
showing how
Roman military
sandals were cut
from a single
piece of leather.

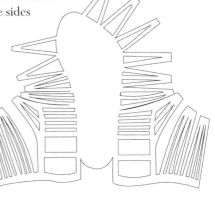

Britons did not become citizens until 212 when an imperial edict gave citizenship to all freeborn inhabitants of the empire.

Married women wore the *stola*, a looser garment than a tunic. It was ankle-length. They might wear a sleeved tunic underneath it, and below that, a breast band as a brassiere. Over her *stola* a woman could wear a belt or girdle and a shawl or *palla*. This was usually wool and was often draped over her head when she went out because it was risky for a woman to go bareheaded in public. A *mappa* could be used to wipe away dust or perspiration. This was a piece of cloth like a handkerchief, carried in the hand or over the shoulder. Babies were wrapped in swaddling bands.

Cloaks and mantles were worn all over the empire, but especially in the northern provinces. Mantles were worn over the shoulder and around the body; but they had to be held in place. In Britain cloaks were fastened at the shoulder with a pin or brooch, a particularly native touch which meant it was not necessary to hold a hand on a cloak or mantle. A type of brooch known as a *fibula* was popular. This was a strong pin with a shaped head which could take different sinuous forms: palmette, lyre, wave tendrils or even dragonesque. Hoods with short cloaks attached (*cuculli*) were worn in bad weather over ordinary cloaks. The military cloak (*sagum*) had the upper half pinned back during day and was used as a blanket at night. The *paenula* was a thick hooded cloak of wool, felt

Leather bikini trunks, found in London; these belonged to a young girl, possibly an acrobatic dancer.

Beads from a Roman necklace made from jet from Whitby, Yorkshire; found in the Boscombe Down Roman coffin.

48

or leather and worn with a thick scarf. The *byrrus Britannicus* was a heavy cape of wool or skins with a hood attached. It was made in weaving shops on big estates around Venta Icenorum (Caistor by Norwich) or Venta Belgarum (Winchester). After export to other parts of the empire, these items could be sold as quality products.

The northern climate had an effect on shoes and socks as well. Traditional Roman sandals and boots such as the *calceus* and the military sandal (*caligae*) were eventually replaced by the *gallica*, a shoe of northern origin, which had soles built up from several layers, fastened together with hobnails. The *calceus* was an open-toed bootee. It had uppers of cloth or leather, covering the foot. It was worn with the toga. Roman sandals had leather soles without heels. Women's shoes were made from softer leather, often in brighter colours. *Caligae* had straps across foot and instep with thongs above the ankle; they were cut out from a single piece of leather. Their soles had hobnails for grip and to prevent them quickly becoming worn out. Evidence from Vindolanda confirms that even soldiers wore socks in cold northern conditions.

Coins found in Dorchester span the period of Roman Britain.

Left: A Roman hairpin made from carved bone, found in Dorchester. The figure is of the winged cherub Cupid, the Roman god of love.

Overleaf: An aerial reconstruction of the forum at the heart of Silchester, with a single entrance, shops around the side of the square, and stalls in the middle. Artwork by Pete Urmston.

TRANSPORT

TRAVEL, FOR MOST PEOPLE, meant walking on Roman Britain's well-made roads. Many of these were built by the Roman army as it advanced into new territory. By the end of the first century, the Romans had already built eight-thousand miles of roads in Britain, including over 1,200 miles during the northern campaign of AD 82. Their original purpose was military: to ensure that troops and supplies could move, at first, from the Channel ports of Rutupiae (Richborough) and Dubris (Dover) to the military centres at London, Colchester, and the forts on the front line. The road from Exeter to Lincoln linked two legionary fortresses, and also marked the frontier of the original province. This road is now known as the Fosse Way although the Roman name for it is unknown. Later the network was expanded by other roads that served economic purposes, linking production centres such as the lead mines of the Mendips in the southwest, or the potteries of the Nene Valley (near present-day Peterborough), with administrative centres like Silchester and the ports. Local roads connected villas, temples, farms and villages to larger roads and market towns. It is likely that no village or farm was more than some seven miles from a purpose-built road of some kind.

Roman roads affected the life of ordinary Britons right from the outset. The vast majority of Britons still lived their entire lives within a few miles of where they were born but even so they benefited from the movement of goods along the network of roads. They might even have been involved in building them. The roads were mainly built by the soldiers themselves but they were assisted by civilians conscripted into forced labour. They were given the unskilled tasks of clearing and digging the ground, cutting trees and collecting building materials, usually local stone or gravel.

Before the Romans arrived the roads and paths had mostly just connected fields and hamlets, but there were also a few longer trade routes such as the Icknield Way that ran along the Chilterns into Norfolk.

Opposite:
A Roman road across the Pennines in Lancashire.

Most were earth tracks following natural contours. The Romans ignored these existing roads, and laid their own roads out straight unless there was a natural obstacle in the way. The routes were worked out by parties of trained surveyors, who were called *agrimensores* or *gromafici*, because they used an instrument known as a *groma*. This was a wooden staff from which two pairs of lead weights were suspended at right angles to each other. They aligned the weights of one pair to lay out the route of the new road between sighting landmarks. Small hills were cut through, and wet ground covered by causeways, or timber embankments.

An area up to 90 feet wide was cleared, and two ditches dug in the centre. The earth was piled up between them to form an embankment, which the Romans called the *agger*. This could be up to 45–50 feet wide and 4–5 feet high. Then, there were three layers of stones, with the largest at the bottom and gravel on the top. The form of construction was so substantial that stretches of Roman road have survived up to the present, for example one beside Stane Street not far from Bignor Roman villa in West Sussex. They only occasionally needed repair or resurfacing. Away from military areas, maintenance became the responsibility of towns or local landowners. As well as troops, horses and pack animals, the roads were used by vehicles laden with goods and supplies.

The most common vehicle was the two-wheeled horse-drawn cart, known as *cissium* or *essedium*, or the four-wheeled cart, known as the *raeda*, for freight, or *carruca* for passengers, which might be ox-drawn. A *carruca dormitoria* was fitted for sleeping, eating or writing. The harness consisted of shafts and traces; snaffle, curbs and bits. The cart bodies varied from flat platforms for freight to wicker baskets or wooden box-like structures. In Italy and Rome itself, wheeled traffic was not allowed into towns during the day but this rule did not extend to the provinces.

Cross-section of the *agger*, the Roman form of road construction; the word comes from a verb meaning 'to heap up'.

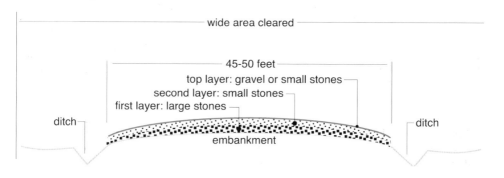

wide area cleared

45-50 feet

top layer: gravel or small stones

second layer: small stones

first layer: large stones

ditch

ditch

embankment

Horses and mules had iron shoes but oxen and mules were most frequently used as draft animals. Sometimes, horses and mules used the softer verge. The Romans rode without stirrups but with saddles, equipped with cantles at each corner to support the rider. Riders such as imperial messengers had to cover many miles each day. A Roman mile was one thousand military paces (1,620 yards). Stone mileposts with the emperor's name inscribed on top gave the distances marked in Roman numerals.

Reconstruction of a four-wheeled cart, or *raeda*.

Hostels known as *mansiones* were built a day's ride, 20–30 miles, apart. In a town they were usually just inside one of the main gates. Additional stables were positioned 6–16 miles apart so imperial messengers could change their hard-ridden (fast) horses. Army and government officials were allowed to use a *mansio* provided they had a permit but they were really intended for the *cursus publicus*: an imperial messenger who acted as a despatch rider, identifiable by the feathers on his spear. They followed road maps such as the Antonine itinerary. This was a collection of routes from all over the empire for use by travelling officials. Because it was intended for the delivery of messages to officials like tax collectors, it directed the riders to take routes via the better-populated areas rather than taking more direct routes through less-populated, areas.

Reconstruction of a two-wheeled cart or *essedium*, modified to carry amphorae.

Roads ideally crossed rivers at shallow crossing points where the river-bed was firm and the banks were passable. Such fords might have paving or timber kerbs to make crossing easier. In some cases, though, bridges were constructed on piles or boats. At Castor, near Northampton, and Newcastle the wooden roadway was supported by stone piers. Corbridge in Northumberland near Hadrian's Wall had cut-waters upstream. The London–

Model of a Roman port, based on archaeological excavations. It shows the development of London ports during the Roman period.

Silchester road crossed the Thames at Pontes (Staines); the Roman name means bridges. Waterways were vital for carrying heavy goods such as grain from East Anglia to the garrison at Lindum (Lincoln). Canals were dug to connect towns to rivers. This made Eboracum (York) and Glevum (Gloucester) into inland ports. The legionary bases of Isca Silurum (Caerleon) and Deva (Chester) were probably not only supplied by sea, but also acted as ports of entry for goods destined for a wider market. Sea-going vessels could meet riverine traffic at major cities and even smaller towns such as Ouenta (Caister on Sea, Norfolk) which developed after AD 125 for trade with the Rhine, in glass, pottery and millstones.

Opposite bottom: Model of a Roman bridge over the Rhine (built by Julius Caesar in 55 BC).

The Britons had used coracles and hollowed-out logs for work such as ferrying across rivers. Coracles were light, round boats made from leather skins stretched over light wooden frames. The Romans replaced them with clinker-built boats (with overlapping planks on a wooden frame). River barges and ferries were developed into flat-bottomed craft with curved bows and raised sterns, propelled by oars and guided by a steersman. A barge found near the mouth of the Fleet river was 55 feet long, 22 feet wide, 7 feet deep with a flat bottom but no keel. The planking of the hull was carvel- (flush) built.

For seagoing the Romans used two types of merchant ship: the *corbita* and the *punto*. The *corbita* had a rounded hull which could hold up to 400 tons of cargo in the hold, access to which was through a hatchway in front of the main mast. The deck and hull were planked. The planking

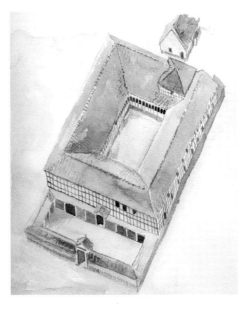

was fastened with wooden dowels. Towards the stern the deck was raised above the level of the main deck. The helmsman stood at the tiller between the deck house and the stern balustrade which surrounded the curved, arched stern and the characteristic swan's-neck ornament. The other type of merchant ship, the *punto* had a projecting bow in front of the stem, resembling the ram of a warship. Both *corbita* and *punto* had steering oars on either side of the stern. These could be raised or lowered. The ships were propelled by square

Above: Illustration of a *mansio*, based on one at Durovigutum, (Godmanchester, where Ermine Street crosses the River Ouse).

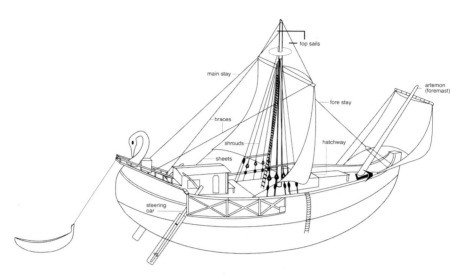

top sails

main stay

artemon
(foremast)

fore stay

braces

shrouds

hatchway

sheets

steering
oar

A Roman
merchant ship, or
corbita.

linen mainsails suspended from wooden yards, and pairs of triangular topsails. At the stem a short mast projected forwards like a stubby bowsprit, fitted with a small sail suspended from a yard. This helped the ship sail closer to the wind. Merchant ships were manned by a small crew, sometimes as few as six seamen. They controlled the sails from the deck with ropes. Halyards were used to raise and lower the yard, and the sails were furled by raising and lowering them, and tying the excess with brails, or short threads. Braces attached to the ends of the yard allowed the sailors to adjust the angle of the yard according to wind conditions, while sheets secured the lower corners of the sails. Such merchant ships usually carried a small rowing-boat to act as a tender for towing purposes or ferrying people ashore.

Ships like the *corbita* sailed up to riverine ports like Londinium on the incoming tide and left on an outgoing tide. They were towed or pulled into the dockside where they unloaded and loaded their cargo. Waiting ships anchored in the river. The docks were wooden structures built out into the river. Warehouses to store goods lined the riverfront.

When at sea, the ships kept the coast in sight wherever possible and anchored at night. A naval fleet attached to the province had as its main role the protection of the cross-Channel route to Gaul. Few ships sailed during winter (from November to March) because the weather was very often too bad to sail. The sailing season was from April until October.

LEISURE

FOR MOST PEOPLE, the only respite from daily work was sleep or enforced inactivity because of bad weather. In towns there were more opportunities for relaxation and entertainment. The Romans provided entertainment for the masses as part of the attempts to win their support and approval.

Story telling was enjoyed by ordinary people in both town and country. Itinerant storytellers called bards sang traditional epic tales, accompanied by an instrument such as a lyre. People gathered around the fire of a roundhouse on a winter's evening or outside in the summer. Stories from Roman history or classical myths might be told in homes more inclined to Rome.

Although no one took weekends or regular days off, there were many festivals which served as holidays. In addition, special days were reserved for the theatre and for games. Seasonal festivals were highly significant for societies based on agriculture because they marked the important seasons such as spring planting, midsummer, harvest and midwinter. The calendar recorded months but not weeks. Every ninth day was a market day (*nundinae*). Like the Celtic calendar, the Roman year was divided into lunar months: from each new moon to the next. By the time the Romans came to Britain, their calendar had become the familiar sequence: Januarius, Februarius, Martius, Aprilis, Maius, Junius, Julius, Augustus, September, October, November and December. They even took account of the 'leap' years, adding an extra day to February every fourth year. The Britons had named their months after trees: Beth (Birch), Luis (Rowan), Nion (Ash), Fearn (Alder),

Bronze model of a *biga*, a racing chariot drawn by two horses, first century BC. Chariot racing was the most popular entertainment in the Roman empire.

Saille (Willow), Huath (Hawthorn), Duir (Oak), Tinne (Holly), Coll (Hazel), Muin (Vine), Gort (Ivy), Ngetal (Reed) and Ruis (Elder).

Rather than numbering each day of the month, the Romans counted them as days before three named days: the Kalends (the new moon, or first day of the month), the Nones (the first quarter-moon, the fifth or seventh day), and the Ides (full moon, thirteenth or fifteenth day).

Each day of the year was categorized as either *comitialis* (lucky days when the popular assembly could meet), *fastus* (lucky days, lawful for business) or *nefastus* (unlucky days when nothing new should be started); often these days were appointed for religious festivals). Some days were deemed so unlucky that nothing (including religious observances) should be done on them. Depending on the time of day, a few days were both lucky and unlucky.

The Britons' priests, the Druids, also kept track of the calendar but Romans regarded them as leaders of resistance to Roman rule and wanted to diminish their influence. They tried to achieve this by their policy of *interpretatio*. This involved relating their own deities and rituals to the local ones. For example, they merged traditional festivals such as Samhain, at the end of the harvest, with their own festivals of Feralia and Pomona. Pomona was the Roman goddess of fruit and trees. The tradition of bobbing for apples developed from ancient rites in honour of Pomona and a Druidic rite associated with water. Seasonal occasions such as the first day of spring made a real difference to the lives of ordinary people. The Britons celebrated the beginning of spring on the 1st or 2nd of February. It was known as Imbolc or Oimelc which means 'ewe's milk'. The Britons' milk came mainly from sheep and goats. Because of the birth of spring lambs and kids, this date meant the return of fresh milk. The spring equinox, when day and night are both twelve hours long, was known as Alban eiler or 'spring hare'. Hares were native to Britain and the kind of game most accessible to ordinary Britons. The next festival was Beltane which celebrated midsummer and fertility. People celebrated by lighting big bonfires and walking round them holding rowan branches or wearing hawthorn branches as symbols of fertility. Young men leapt over the fires. Ordinary people ate well in celebration: it might be one of the few occasions on which they ate meat because it was associated with feasting and religious sacrifices.

Midwinter brought another mixture of native and Roman traditions. The Romans celebrated one of their most distinctive festivals, the Saturnalia, at Yule or the winter solstice. For five days they turned the established social order upside down and allowed activities such as gambling; masters waited on their servants and in each household everyone had to obey the king of the Saturnalia. Whoever threw the highest score on the dice was chosen as king of the Saturnalia. The Romans gave gifts to each other and adorned their homes with greenery. In Britain they used holly and ivy which were used to make wreaths in the Yuletide celebrations. Freedmen wore colourful conical hats during the Saturnalia.

Roman dice.

Both the Britons and the Romans enjoyed gambling despite the fact that it was illegal except during the Saturnalia. They made bets on both formal and informal sporting events as simple as the toss of a coin. The calls were heads (*capitae*) or ships (*naves*). The Romans introduced dice (*tesserae*) to Britain. They were made of glass, bone, lead or even semi-precious stones such as agate. They were six sided, like ours, with values from one to six marked or inscribed on the faces. In games of chance (*alea*) you threw three dice at a time. They also played knucklebones or *tali*. Four *tali* were thrown at a time, the highest throw was when all four were different (the Venus throw).

Board games were popular: ordinary people just scratched the board on a tile or the pavement. *Duodecim scripta* (twelve lines) was a form of backgammon with bone counters. Players threw three dice. *Ludus lutrunculum* or 'soldiers' was a game like drafts but with only eight squares in each direction: pieces were trapped between two opposing pieces. Forward and backward moves were allowed. The winner was the player who captured the most pieces.

Games could be played on boards scratched on a piece of clay or a tile.

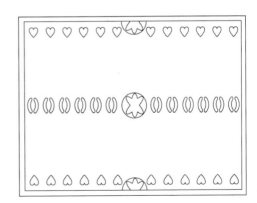

The board for *duodecim scripta*.

The Roman amphitheatre at Caerleon; the arena and parts of the original earth banks, entrances, recesses and stone retaining walls are still clearly visible.

Babies could be amused by hinged pieces of wood or clappers, rattles with bells or terracotta animals with pebbles inside in the shape of stags, horses or pigs. Girls had dolls made of wood, bone or baked clay, sometimes with hinged joints. They could paint or dress them. When the girls married, they dedicated their dolls to Venus. Children also played with hoops and tops, games of leap-frog and blind man's buff. *Trigon* was a popular ball game for three players, catching with one hand and throwing with the other.

The great Roman entertainments such as chariot racing and games with gladiator-fights were staged at towns and forts with a military presence, such as Colchester and Caerleon. Games were held in amphitheatres. Chariot races took place in a type of amphitheatre known as a circus. At first, provincial amphitheatres were built of timber. Later they were rebuilt in stone.

A full day at the games began with a parade by the participants, then warm-up acts like acrobats and jugglers, followed by wild beast fights, with the main acts in the afternoon. In Britain, cheaper acts such as cockfights, juggling, boxing, wrestling and acrobatic turns would have taken up most of the bill. Parades of criminals and public executions, including Christian martyrs, took place at lunchtime. Gladiators were rare in Britain but they were top of the bill if available. They fought in matched pairs in which the advantages and disadvantages of their arms and armour were intended to create an even contest. For example, the heavily armoured *murmillo*, armed with

Diagram of a provincial circus or racetrack.

starting gates

linea alba

Finishing line

a short sword and a shield was pitched against the lighter *retiarius*, armed with only a trident and a weighted net. The *retiarius* was the only gladiator type who fought without a helmet. He had a piece of protective armour on his left shoulder known as a *galerus* but he had to use his speed and agility to evade his opponent. All gladiators fought barefoot. Arenas had surfaces of sand which were raked after each event. Schools of gladiators toured the provinces. The sponsor of the games paid for the gladiators or charioteers.

The biggest sporting events were the chariot races. Souvenir glass beakers found near the sites of circuses are proof of their popularity. There was a permanent circus at Colchester which would have attracted betting both for and against the teams. It was 350 metres (382 yards) long. Temporary courses could have been set up with marker posts, wooden rails and wicker starting gates. Roman chariot races lasted seven laps around a central barrier or *spina*. A distance of two miles was covered. Once the chariots left the starting gates, they raced in separate lanes to the *linea alba* or white line. Once they crossed the *linea alba*, the charioteers could change lanes to try to get on the inside of the 180 degree turns at each end of the course. The chariots were light vehicles like wicker baskets on an axle. They were drawn by either a pair of horses, a *biga*, or a team of four, a *quadriga*. The charioteer wound the reins around his body so he could steer by leaning. If he crashed he was dragged along the ground until he cut himself free with a knife he wore specifically for that purpose.

Replica of a souvenir glass beaker depicting a *quadriga*, after an original found near Colchester.

Beaker depicting a stag and a hind being hunted by hounds, found at Newstead, Melrose.

Crashes were known as shipwrecks (*naufragia*). Racing programmes featured several races in a day. The charioteers belonged to teams, identified by their colours: green, blue, red and white. Individual charioteers could become rich and famous, changing teams or being bought or sold like modern football players. People supported a team rather than individual charioteers.

Theatre was another form of sponsored entertainment which ordinary people could enjoy. There were theatres at St Albans, Colchester and Canterbury. They staged recitals and pantomimes more often than plays. The mimes enacted crude jokes and horseplay based on scenes of everyday life featuring stock characters (*fabula atellana*) such as the clown, grandpa and the dog.

Baths incorporated gymnasia. These were colonnaded courtyards where wrestling and exercising took place before visitors undressed and bathed. In the complex at Caerleon the exercise arena was moved under cover. Some people used visits to the gymnasia and the baths to

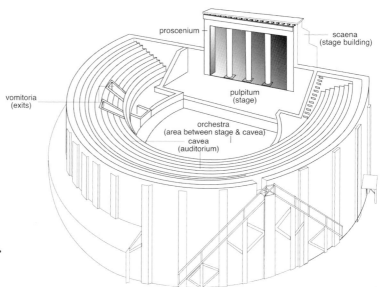

Diagram of a provincial theatre, based on Verulamium (St Albans).

socialise with their friends. Some large bath-houses featured separate sets of baths for men and women; alternatively, men and women would have to use the baths at different times. Public baths were usually built by benefactors so the entrance fee was small. Children, soldiers and sometimes slaves used them for free.

A peregrine falcon, which takes feathered prey.

Both Romans and Britons loved hunting. Ordinary people in the country could go fowling with nets, knocking birds out of trees with jointed rods smeared with bird-lime and the use of traps, nets or bows and arrows. They also went hare coursing, following hunting dogs on foot. The dogs were trained to run down the quarry and bring it to bay or drive it into the nets. Larger prey such as deer and boar were restricted to those with greater means; for example, Roman officers. Ordinary people took part as huntsmen, beaters or dog handlers. Hunters used large mastiff-like dogs to tackle boar or stag and the *vertragus*, a fast dog, like a greyhound, for hares. The dogs lead the huntsmen to the prey where the huntsmen killed it with knives and hunting spears. Bear were hunted in Britain but these were exported for beast fights elsewhere in the empire. Falconry or hunting with birds of prey involved ordinary people who caught, trained and looked after the birds for the elite who flew them and ate the prey. In Britain they used peregrine falcons to bring down feathered prey like pigeon. Hawks took furred prey like rabbits.

Until they conquered Gaul the Romans had not come across salmon fishing but Britons and Romans both fished for salmon and trout in rivers like the Severn. The writer Ausonius remarked that the Britons fished for sport: fly-fishing with rod and line made from twisted horsehair with bait made from earthworms, ants, pork fat and shellfish.

EDUCATION AND SOCIAL SERVICE

B OTH THE BRITONS and the Romans valued knowledge and education, but the great difference between their cultures was that the Britons had an oral tradition and the Romans were a literate society. The Britons learnt by memorising what they had heard. The Romans wrote it down. Although the Romans despised the Druids, Julius Caesar noted that students of Druidism spent up to twenty years on their studies, and that they were 'diligent in learning by heart' and did not 'let their memories rust'. Strabo described the Druids as a lower order of bards or storytellers and a higher order of augurs who presided over religious ceremonies. Their tradition of oral learning allowed them to keep their doctrines from becoming widely known as well as training the memory.

The Britons' language had no written form but Latin was the language not just of the army but also that of trade, commerce and law. Both official business and personal affairs involved written documents such as records and letters. So the Romans introduced reading and writing to Britain. The Romans had a considerable literary heritage. They had also developed easy and cheap forms of written communication. These ranged from books in scroll form to scratching writing on fragments of pottery. Wise governors of Britain such as Agricola realised that education would help to keep the province peaceful. He encouraged the chieftains of the Britons to have their sons learn Latin and have a formal education in the Roman way. The result was that 'a dislike of the Latin language was replaced by a passion to speak it'. This was similar to the way in which, many years later, the public schools became academies for the rich where learning Latin would make the sons of landowners better estate managers.

Under the *pax Romana*, ordinary people such as traders, shopkeepers and craftsmen as well as soldiers could read and write. They and their wives needed to keep records and communicate with correspondents elsewhere.

A reproduction of a writing-desk with scrolls and other writing materials.

A child's formal education usually began at the age of seven. Until they were twelve, either they would have studied at home with a tutor, or at a school which charged fees. Schools in Roman towns were often small rooms off the forum containing a chair for the teacher and benches or stools for the pupils. Richer children were brought to school by pedagogues, slaves who acted as servants and guardians. The pedagogues might have been educated themselves in a *pedagogium*, a schoolroom for slaves in a large house. Pupils learnt reading, writing and arithmetic. The limitations of the Roman numeric system limited progress to learning multiplication tables by rote and recitation.

Wax and wooden writing tablets, *styli*, pen and smoother. The tablet (top left) is sealed.

Pumicing papyrus to make it a better writing surface.

They also learnt to use an abacus, a simple counting device. They learnt the alphabet by writing on tablets, parchment, papyri or even scratching on pottery shards. Ordinary people 'left school' after this stage.

The next stage of a formal education, from the age of twelve to fifteen, was attending a *grammaticus* who taught preparation for public life. This involved learning the art of speaking and writing Latin and Greek properly, with knowledge of literature, poetry, history and philosophy. To speak Latin and Greek properly a pupil should avoid colloquialisms or antiquated phraseology. The pupil ought to use clear diction that was both accurate and elegant. A small number of pupils went further to study with a teacher of rhetoric as preparation for the highest positions such as entering the senate or standing for public office. This involved learning a series of gestures to express emotions such as disbelief or a request for silence.

The Romans used a versatile piece of equipment in the form of a wax tablet. These were wooden tablets with raised edges which contained a layer of wax on which one wrote with a metal pen or stylus. The writing in the wax could be erased by smoothing the wax with the other end of the stylus or a smoother which was broad and flat for this purpose. Wax tablets usually had two or more leaves bound by leather thongs like a book. Important documents like wills could be sealed. The Romans also wrote in ink on wooden tablets (*tilia*) as well as parchment and papyri. Parchment was specially prepared thin sheepskin. It was expensive and was used for books and important documents. Books took the

form of a number of scrolls in a cylindrical case known as a *capsa*. Papyrus was made from specially prepared reeds. The sheets benefited from being smoothed with pumice-stones. Papyrus was not native to Britain where wooden tablets were more commonly used for records and letters.

Elsewhere in the empire, *tilia* were made from lime wood (*tilia* means lime), but in Britain they were made from birch or alder and occasionally oak. They were cut from wood and the largest was the size of a postcard. They were usually written on in two columns, then scored down the middle and folded. Several wooden tablets could be laced together, in concertina fashion. The address was written on the back of the right-hand leaf.

There were two main kinds of Latin handwriting: capital letters and cursive script. Our capital letters derive from the Roman ones. The Romans used abbreviations, such as 'm' for *modius*, and even shorthand. Letters or records on wooden tablets were usually written in cursive script. Cursive letters were similar to ancient Greek and sloped upwards from left to right. The main text was sometimes written by a scribe who was a paid professional or a literate slave. The correspondent often wrote the opening address and the valediction themselves. Both those in the army and in trade were literate to

Wooden writing tablet from Vindalonda, c. 100. The collection of about 1,000 letters discovered here in the 1970s, has offered a unique window into life on the frontiers of the Roman World.

The Roman alphabet written in cursive script on a wax tablet.

Above:
The inscription on a gravestone from Bath. It is dedicated to Lucius Vitellius Tancinus, an auxiliary cavalryman.

the extent of keeping records which they wrote themselves. Centurions and even rank-and-file soldiers had to write documents such as strength reports, supply and leave requests (*commeatus*).

Inscriptions on stone were the most visible sign of Roman literate culture. They were sited in plain view of ordinary people whether they could read or not. Capital inscriptions were mainly made to commemorate building projects, or on altars or dedications to the gods or emperors. Individuals could jointly commission an altar; for example, at Caerleon, one was inscribed: 'to Salus the Queen from Publius Salienius Thalamus son of Publius of the Maecian voting tribe from Hadria prefect of the second Augusta legion with his sons Ampeianus and Lucilianus gave this gift'. They also commemorated family members. On the edge of the site of the baths, a dedication to 'Fortuna and Bonus Eventus' was set up by a husband and wife, Cornelius Castus and Julia Belismious. Civil communities recorded public or private building schemes and dedications. They publicised laws and decisions, celebrated careers and achievements and recorded votive offerings and other religious acts as well as marking burials.

The range of written communications varied from makers' marks on objects such as pottery to graffiti on buildings. News was sometimes posted in the forum in the form of gazettes, known as *Acta*. Coins carried written messages on their faces. They added to the prestige of the emperor by showing his name and likeness. Stone inscriptions were cut in the eponymous capital letters which were cumbersome and expensive. This led to abbreviations such as DM on a tombstone, which stood for *Dis Manibus* ('to the spirits of the dead'). Symbols were also inscribed, such as the chevron mark which meant a century (a company of 100 soldiers) or a centurion.

Ordinary people were more likely to be responsible for writing curse tablets than stone inscriptions. Curse tablets or *defixiones* were small sheets of lead, inscribed with messages from individuals who

Reproduction of a curse tablet.

wanted to make gods or spirits act on their behalf, or against others with whom they had a grievance. On curse tablets we can read the thoughts of provincials and non-citizens, even women and slaves. They expressed their ill-will and violent attitudes against others who had harmed them or from whom they wanted something such as a favourable outcome at the chariot races. A common curse was against whoever had stolen someone's cloak. The letters and lines were written back to front and magical words and symbols were added to give them additional potency. Finally they might be thrown into water at places where the gods or spirits could be contacted such as Bath or Uley. Alternatively they were buried, either with the dead or at the turning post of a circus.

The only social service was fire-fighting. Fires were common in towns because people cooked over open fires and heated their homes with braziers. Timber-framed buildings with thatched roofs easily caught fire. In both St Albans and Wroxeter the forum burnt down.

An astonishing 2,000-year-old stone plaque shows the oldest Roman naming of London.

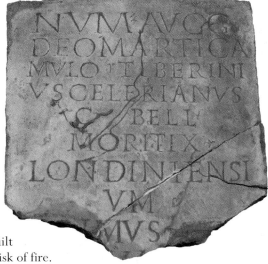

Rome had its own force of firemen, known as Vigiles, but, in the provinces, local fire brigades were supposed to patrol at night. At best they were equipped only with axes, fire buckets and grass or esparto mats so, once fires took hold, they spread rapidly. The only effective tactic to prevent fires spreading was to pull down adjacent buildings to create a fire-break. If someone pulled down his neighbour's house, he was not liable for damages if it was deemed to be in the common good. Timber-framed buildings could be rebuilt relatively quickly. Large bath-houses were often built outside the town itself to reduce the risk of fire.

HEALTH

G OOD HEALTH DEPENDS UPON good sanitary conditions. In towns and military centres this in turn depended on the supply of clean water. Towns in Roman Britain relied on wells and springs rather than aqueducts. Fresh water was also collected from nearby rivers or streams in open conduits. Lincoln had two: one for the baths, the other for public use. For use at home, water had to be collected from the well or local source and carried back in buckets. This would have been a daily chore. Most of the available water was used by the bath houses, fed by lead pipes at Bath and York. Bath was exceptional because it had a natural hot spring, which still produces over a million litres of water per day at 120 degrees F (46 degrees C). Both Britons and Romans regarded this as miraculous and endowed with healing properties. Healing was regarded as a spiritual blessing and places with health-giving benefits, such as Bath, were dedicated to gods or spirits. At Bath this was the local deity Sulis whom the Romans identified with Minerva. They called Bath, Aquae Sulis (waters of Sulis) although the deity was known as Sulis Minerva. By AD 76 they had developed the hot spring into a baths-and-temple complex which included the Great Bath: a roofed swimming pool, lined with lead, filled by mineral water from the hot spring.

There were other healing centres or sanctuaries at Lydney Park, Gloucester and Buxton, Derbyshire (Aquae Arnemetiae). The sanctuary at Lydney Park was dedicated to Mars Nodens. Mars, the Roman god of war, was also associated with

The great bath at Aquae Sulis. The pillar bases are Roman but the columns were built in the eighteenth century. The bath is lead-lined and is fed by naturally hot water.

healing. Nodens was a Celtic deity whose devotees left votive offerings. These were small bronze representations of parts of their bodies which they wanted to be healed such as arms or legs. They dropped the votive offerings into the pools.

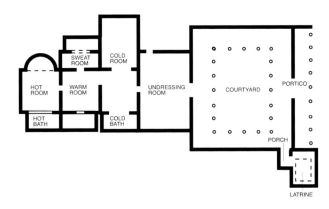

Above: Plan of a bath complex.

Regular visits to the baths improved even ordinary townspeople's physical and mental welfare. Visitors undressed in the *apodyterium* where the bathers left their clothes in niches in the wall. It was wise to give the attendant a small tip to look after your clothes, as otherwise they could be stolen. Then they rubbed olive oil over their bodies before exercising in the *palaestra*. The normal Roman design for this was a colonnaded open-air space but in Britain the weather was not always good enough: at Caerleon a basilica was added as an indoor gymnasium to the military baths complex. After exercising, running, wrestling or using weights, visitors to the baths began with a dip in a cold plunge before entering the *tepidarium* or warm room. The baths were heated under the floors by a hypocaust: built-in cavities that allowed hot air to circulate under the floors and through ducts in the walls. The floors became so hot that the bathers had to wear wooden clogs. Bath-houses were sometimes laid out so that bathers could choose which room they wanted to use next. Rather than big baths in each room, hot or cold water was available for bathers to mix to the temperature they wanted before emptying it over themselves. After the *tepidarium*, they could take another cold plunge or enter the hot room or *caldarium*. The hottest room, the *sudatorium*, was similar to a sauna. Bathers could retrace their steps before a final cold plunge to close the pores.

Below: Plan of a hypocaust under a bathhouse, showing the flow of hot air.

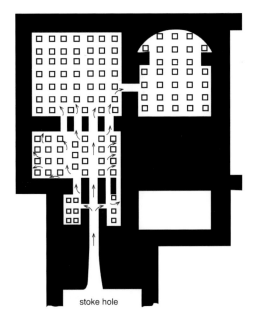

stoke hole

Detail of *pilae* still supporting part of the original floor of a hot room, or *caldarium* (see the plan of the bathhouse hypocaust on the previous page).

Dirt and moisture were scraped off with a curved bronze implement known as a *strigil*. This removed a layer of dead skin as well as any residue of oil and sweat. Water and scrapings went into leaf-shaped drain-holes in the floor. Finally attendants offered massages and other services such as manicures or hair-plucking. Bathers could then sleep, eat snacks such as sausages or shellfish, or gamble and socialise.

In a rural environment people had to make do with more primitive washing arrangements, heating water in a cauldron over the fire or washing in a stream. The Britons used soap made from lye. Lye is made from water filtered through wood ash. This produces a highly caustic liquid. The liquid or lye was then mixed with lard, made from pig fat. The mixture was boiled and stirred for hours with a long-handled paddle until the paddle stood up in it. It was then allowed to cool before being cut into pieces for use.

Despite their attractions baths created problems. They used a great deal of water which carried sewage from their latrines back to the nearest stream or river. Most town drains combined sewage and surface water. The drains also had to carry away animal waste and night soil left in the street. No one was aware of micro-organisms so polluted water could only be detected by taste or smell. Cesspits dug

The remains of a Roman bath-house near North Wraxall, Wiltshire. There were two main phases of building for the bath-house. In the foreground is the 'frigidarium' (cold bath) of the second phase of building.

near wells could pollute the water supply, so lining the sides of wells was deemed necessary and it was best to draw the water from the bottom rather than the sides of a well. At Silchester and London, wells were lined with the wooden barrels used to import wine. Rural communities also emptied their latrines into cesspits which had to be filled in when they became either full or unpleasant.

Wooden clogs for walking on the hot floors of a bathhouse, oil flask & sponge stick.

Public latrines were built in towns and military centres. These were buildings containing stone or wooden benches with openings for defecation. There were no stalls and the tunic preserved modesty while seated. The latrines were built over deep trenches or the cesspit itself. There was an additional keyhole-shaped opening at the front. This allowed the user to clean him- or herself with the Roman equivalent of toilet paper, a natural sea-sponge on a stick. A communal sponge-stick was available in a bowl of vinegar but it was preferable to bring your own. In Britain these had to be imported so they were a necessary expense for an urban craftsman's family, as were bronze bath sets containing strigils, tweezers and other implements.

Medical assistance was available in towns and military centres. The Roman army provided care for its soldiers but everyone else had to pay for a doctor. Alternatively, people went to a temple to be healed or even get a tooth pulled. The army doctors were non-combatant orderlies who cared for the sick and wounded. Only legionary fortresses had hospitals. Roman medicine followed the Greek tradition of Hippocrates. Diagnosis was based on restoring the balance of the four humours or elements: sanguine (air), phlegmatic (water), melancholic (earth) and choleric (fire). Imbalances of the humours were often treated with enemas and emetics such as mustard mixed with salt as a warming agent to help digestion.

From their battlefield experience, the Romans also developed their surgery. This included treatment for broken noses and collar-bones, the setting of broken arms, legs and fingers and their immobilisation with bandages and splints. In the army two *medici* were attached to each legion. As well as amputation, they were capable of operations such as trepanning to relieve concussion. They also offered remedial treatments and first aid such as tourniquets to prevent loss of blood. Vinegar was

The latrine building in the Roman fort at Housesteads. There is a central pavement with basins on it and a shallow drain on either side. Beyond this is a pit (in shadow) over which rows of wooden stalls were placed. The system was flushed by rainwater and there was no privacy.

used as an antiseptic. Honey was used to keep open wounds clean (it is an anti-bacterial agent). After a cut or wound had been stitched, egg-white could be applied to help close cuts as it stretches the skin. They also used bleeding for problems like headaches.

Ordinary people had to rely on folk remedies such as plants with healing properties or traditions like prayers and offerings for recovery. Eye infections were common. Travelling oculists treated them with salves. These were soluble sticks of ointment which were stamped with the trade mark of the oculist. They could be made into treatments such as a vinegar lotion for running eyes, drops for dim sight and poppy ointment for inflammation. Oral hygiene was bad due to decay from consumption of fermented carbohydrates. Bread made from stone-ground flour wore down their teeth. However, they were able to use freshly squeezed juice from sorrel leaves to make an effective mouthwash and benefited from chewing its roots.

For pain, ordinary people had to rely on remedies such as henbane, mandrake and hemlock. They also used plants with healing properties including Good King Henry, self-heal, deadly nightshade and St John's wort. Good King Henry has juicy leaves which are rich in iron, calcium and vitamin C. Deadly nightshade

Roman surgical instruments.

can be used as a painkiller or a sedative. St John's wort has anti-bacterial properties. Doctors used 'poppy tears', an opiate made from the latex or sap of poppies. When poppies are cut, the latex comes out in brown drops, known as 'tears of Demeter' (the earth goddess). Chives were good for sore throats and blood. Rose petals were used to make eye ointments. Valerian petals were sprinkled on beds to bring deep sleep. Coriander seeds and leaves were eaten to treat flatulence.

Many people suffered from poor diet and from carrying heavy loads or accidents such as misdirected hammer blows or slips when ploughing. The tiniest cut opened the possibility of a life-threatening infection. Many children died during childhood from diseases or infections. An inscription was dedicated to a girl who was married aged thirteen but died at the age of nineteen. She had six children but only three of them were still alive when she died. The average height of men was five foot six, that of women five foot one. Life expectancy was not much older than forty for men and thirty-six for women. One of the attractions of eastern religions such as Christianity and Mithraism was the possibility of an afterlife which neither the official state religion of Rome nor the Celtic deities offered. An inscription on the tombstone of a young woman buried in York proclaimed faith in life after death: '*Soror ave, vivas in Deo*' (Hail sister, live in God).

The fourth-century mosaic, thought to represent Christ, from the Roman villa at Hinton St Mary.

PLACES TO VISIT

NATIONAL TRUST SITES

For National Trust sites, go to www.nationaltrust.org.uk and search for the
relevant site.

Hadrian's Wall and Housesteads Fort, Bardon Mill, Hexham, Northumberland
NE47 6NN

Britain's most famous Roman remain, and its best preserved frontier
fort, attractively interpreted. There are many other separate sites and
forts the length of the wall, some of which are listed below.

Letocetum Roman Baths and Museum, Watling Street, Wall, nr Lichfield,
Staffordshire WS14 0AW

Bathhouse of a Roman staging post (mansio) on Watling Street.

ENGLISH HERITAGE

For English Heritage sites, go to www.english-heritage.org.uk and search
for the relevant site.

Carrawburgh Temple of Mithras, Simonburn, Northumberland

A temple dedicated to the god Mithras, the sun god whose cult was
popular among soldiers of the Roman legions.

Chester Roman Amphitheatre, Vicars Lane, Chester

The largest Roman amphitheatre in Britain, used for entertainment and
training by the 20th Legion, based at the fortress of Deva (Chester).

Chesters Roman Fort, Chollerford, Northumberland, NE46 4EU

The best-preserved Roman cavalry fort in Britain, Chesters guarded
the point where Hadrian's Wall crossed the River South Tyne.

Cirencester Roman Amphitheatre, Cotswold Avenue, Cirencester, Gloucestershire

Able to hold over 8,000, bear-, dog- and bull-baiting were probably
practised, as well as public executions and gladiatorial contests.

Silchester Roman city, Silchester, Hampshire

The Romans reused the Atrebate site to create Calleva Attrebatum. The
town walls and the amphitheatre are open to visitors all year.

CADW (Wales)

For CADW sites, go to www.cadw.wales.gov.uk and search for the
relevant site.

Caerleon Amphitheatre, Barracks and Baths

Remains of the baths, amphitheatre, barracks and fortress wall. The
museum contains ephemera and a reconstructed interior of a barracks.

Caerwent Roman Town

Tribal capital of the Silures (Venta Silurum) with high fourth-century
walls. Excavated houses, the forum-basilica and a temple remain.

OTHERS

Museum of London, London Wall, London, EC2Y 5HN

Museum with a fine collection of Roman artefacts from all aspects of Londinium life, and many reconstructed room sets.

Arbeia Roman Fort and Museum, Baring St, South Shields, Tyne and Wear, NE33 2BB

Arbeia was the supply base for the forts along the Wall. Excavated remains, and reconstructions of original buildings can be seen.

Butser Ancient Farm, Chalton, Waterlooville, Hampshire, PO8 0BG

A working Iron-Age farm with animals and crops of the type grown during the Roman period, round houses and a Roman villa .

Roman Lincoln and *The Collection*, Danes Terrace, Lincoln, LN2 1LP

The East and North Gates (Newport Arch) of the Roman walls remain in the town. The museum (the Collection) has many Roman artefacts.

Lunt Roman Fort, Coventry Rd, Coventry, West Midlands, CV8 3AJ

Only the ditches of this fort remain. The wooden gatehouse, ramparts, a granary and a gyrus (horse-training centre) have been reconstructed.

The Roman Baths, Stall Street, Bath, BA1 1LZ

The Roman baths were used from about AD 80–400. A museum houses finds from the excavations, including a giant stone Medusa's head.

British Museum, Great Russell St, London, WC1B 3DG

A collection of treasures from Roman Britain including mosaics, silverware, ephemera and models of forts and settlements.

Corinium Museum, Park Street, Cirencester, Gloucestershire, GL7 2BX

This museum tells the story of the Roman town of Corinium. A wealth of finds are displayed, a Roman town-house interior, and mosaic floor.

Verulamium Museum, St Michael's St, St Albans, Hertfordshire, AL3 4SW

Several parts of the site can be viewed: the hypocaust, the theatre and the remains of the city walls and London gate.

Fishbourne Roman Palace and Gardens, Salthill Rd, Fishbourne, Chichester, Sussex, PO19 3QR.

The remains of a palatial Roman building of the first century AD. View unique mosaics and the replanted garden.

London Guildhall, Gresham St, London EC2

The site of London's gladiatorial amphitheatre is picked out in lights beneath the City's medieval hall.

Roman Vindolanda, Bardon Mill, Hexham, Northumberland, NE47 7JN

The fort near the Wall where the Vindolanda letters were found, there is now a major Roman Army Museum and extensive excavations.

Welwyn Roman Baths, Welwyn Bypass, Hertfortshire, AL6 9HT

A typical domestic bathhouse, part of a third-century villa complex, preserved in a vault underneath the A1(M).

INDEX